nature meditations

JOURNAL

mindful practices and restorative activities
inspired by the natural world

Kenya Jackson-Saulters

CHRONICLE BOOKS
SAN FRANCISCO

ISBN 978-1-7972-2515-9

Manufactured in China.

MIX
Paper | Supporting
responsible forestry
FSC™ C008047

Design by Henna Crowner.

10 9 8 7 6 5 4 3 2 1

Chronicle Books publishes distinctive books and gifts. From
award-winning children's titles, bestselling cookbooks, and
eclectic pop culture to acclaimed works of art and design,
stationery, and journals, we craft publishing that's instantly
recognizable for its spirit and creativity. Enjoy our publishing and
become part of our community at www.chroniclebooks.com.

Special quantity discounts are available to corporations and
other organizations. Contact our premiums department at
corporatesales@chroniclebooks.com or at 1-800-759-0190.

Chronicle Books LLC
680 Second Street
San Francisco, California 94107
www.chroniclebooks.com

nature is one of
the greatest teachers
in my life.

As the cofounder of the Outdoor Journal Tour, an organization that creates wellness events for women in outdoor spaces, I have spent countless hours leading people through transformative experiences in nature. In doing so, I too have been offered eye-opening lessons—lessons of strength, vulnerability, joy, and sadness. Sometimes, these lessons come easily; other times, they are hard fought.

I was reminded of this on a recent trip to Sedona, Arizona, where my wife and I had gone to celebrate my fortieth birthday in nature. It was the end of a hard year in my life, full of personal challenges and deep inner turmoil. So, unlike my friends, who were excited to celebrate the completion of their own fourth decades, I was anxious and nervous. Plus, I was fast approaching the age that my own mother had been when she passed away. She died when she was only forty-two, and ever since I have been terrified of aging. My trip to Sedona was my attempt to disconnect from my fear of aging and find the joy in celebrating another decade of life.

We chose Sedona because of its energy vortexes. Energy vortexes are natural geomagnetic points that create a swirling energy center radiating from the earth's surface. Sedona is famous for its energy vortexes, the most popular of which is the summit of Cathedral Rock. In fact, the ancient Sinague people believed—as do their descendants, the Navajo and Hopi tribes— that Cathedral Rock was not only an energy vortex but also a holy site. The two rock statues that sit atop the mountain are believed to represent the first man and woman to ever walk the earth. The land is sacred.

Climbing Cathedral Rock felt like the perfect way to celebrate a big milestone in my life. Within the first few steps of the climb, I could feel the energy pulsing through my body. I knew that something special would happen here. I also realized that this hike was not going to submit to me easily. Unlocking its gifts would require me to commit to the challenge and acquiesce to its wisdom. But once I did both, the lessons began to flow.

The first lesson—you can do hard things—came to me during a vertical ascent only minutes into the hike. I stood at the bottom of a crevice in the rock, staring at a 40-foot straight-up climb. Impossibility stared back at me. I had no clue how I would make it. Most people don't. In fact, almost half of the group that had started with us quit at this point. Somehow, though, I found the courage to persist. I dug my shoes into the sandstone and my nails into the rock and hoisted myself up the gap. My heart felt like it was going to burst out of my chest.

It turned out, however, that this was just the first of many harrowing scrambles. Cathedral Rock was riddled with slippery ascents and near-vertical climbs. I often struggled to grab on to the weatherworn handholds. My palms were getting raw and chafed. There were even times when I clawed at the rock and burrowed my toes into the trail only to lose my footing and slide backward, losing ground.

As I got nearer to the top, I noticed that there weren't that many hikers left—and for a moment I felt more alone than I wanted to be. And then came the second lesson: Being alone in nature is an opportunity, not a punishment.

I soon realized that although I was alone, it was not in a bad, scary way. It was in a quiet and powerful way. Being alone in that spot meant that I had to depend on myself to make things happen. And I could depend on myself to make things happen.

"I can do this," I said to myself. "I will do this." I began to pay more attention to the sensations in my body, instead of to the noise in my head. I fixed my attention on the steps ahead of me instead of the 700-foot drop below. This was going to be my fortieth-birthday gift to myself. My whole life, I had played it safe, never challenging myself to push too far out of my current comfort zone. Never completely trusting myself or my body. But today—today was going to be different. I would finish—for me—and for my mom, who hadn't been healthy enough to do any-thing like this when she was this age.

The last few feet to the top were brutal. I spoke to myself out loud while completing the final rocky and winding trail to the summit. "You got this, Kenya. Don't quit."

When I finally reached the top, tears welled up in my eyes. I stopped to look at the view and inhaled the deep cleansing air. I had just completed the hardest hike of my life. Life had been so generous, my body had been so strong, my mind had been so focused—and I was so grateful.

By the time I returned to the bottom—an equally difficult feat—I was covered in dirt and bruises, as well as prickles from the cactus bed I had fallen onto. I had been challenged in every way—mind, body, and spirit. But unlike other times in my life, this time I had chosen not to back down from the challenge. I embraced it. I faced my fears, pushed myself beyond my self-imposed limits, and succeeded.

And therein lay the third and final lesson: Nature offers us opportunities to see ourselves and be ourselves.

I share this story with you to remind you of your own power and to encourage you to lean into your personal strength. Allow nature to be your teacher in the process. Nature is generous in the opportunities it gives us to see ourselves and be ourselves. Experiences in the natural world are reminders that you can depend on you. You can trust yourself. And you are worth the effort.

HOW TO USE
THIS JOURNAL

Not every transformative experience in nature has to be so extreme. There are so many beautiful ways to connect with the magic of the outdoors, whether you're on a walk in the park, gazing out your window at a bird, or simply closing your eyes to imagine the sound of a waterfall. This journal is designed to offer you simple ways to engage with the power of the natural world through outdoor experiences, visualizations, meditations, and more. In the following pages, you'll discover a range of meditative journaling prompts to encourage mindfulness, calm, and confidence. The prompts are organized into the following categories:

- **NATURE MEDITATIONS:** Exercises to connect with the healing powers of the natural world.

- **WALKING THOUGHTS:** Questions to encourage mindful reflection and introspection while you're walking outdoors.

- **MESSAGES FROM THE EARTH:** Prompts to bring your awareness to nature's enduring beauty and wisdom.

- **STRENGTHENING AFFIRMATIONS:** Nature-inspired affirmations to help you strengthen your body and empower your mind.

You'll also discover short activities at the end of each category that offer you ways to deepen your connection to the outdoors. Each activity is followed by a reflection prompt so that you can process the experience.

I encourage you to make this journal your own. Flip through to find the prompts and activities that resonate in the moment you are in. Bring the journal with you on a hike, or on a walk through a local park. Use it as a tool to try new things and push yourself out of your comfort zone. Take it with you when you are about to do something hard. Crack it open in celebration afterward. Sit with it while you contemplate the plans you have for your life. Reread the prompts and your responses to remind yourself of who you really are, both when you are at your best and when you are shaking in your boots as you pursue greatness. Allow the pages of this journal to be both your inspiration and a reminder of what lies beneath your surface.

This journal offering is rooted in my work as a coach, an outdoor leader, and a mindfulness practitioner. The practices and activities come from a place of deep emotion, purpose, and life experience. My hope for this work is that it becomes your companion in times of both trial and triumph.

May nature be your teacher.

—Kenya Jackson-Saulters

nature meditations

CONNECT TO YOUR HIGHEST SELF

Find a place to sit or stand comfortably for a few minutes. Close your eyes and envision giant, snowcapped mountains. Imagine the rocky, jagged peaks, jutting into the clouds overhead. Now picture yourself scaling this mountain and reaching its highest point. Imagine the exhilarating feelings and panoramic views from the top of the world. From this place of perspective, contemplate the highest vision you have for yourself. When you've finished, use the space below to journal about what came up. What goals emerged as part of your highest vision? What obstacles do you need to scale so that you can feel on top of the world?

_____

_____

_____

_____

_____

_____

_____

_____

HOME SWEET HOME

Birds build their nests with great intention—selecting the right tree, the right branches, and the right materials to make a safe home. Today, find a quiet place to sit and close your eyes. Picture a bird building a nest high in a tree, skillfully gathering and combining all the components it needs to create its home suspended in the sky. Meditate on this slow, diligent, and purposeful process. Now, imagine that you are building or expanding your own "nest." What components would you gather to do so, and why?

GENTLE SURRENDER

Observing nature can teach us the art of surrendering to change. Just as sand softly melts into the sea at the shore, and light slowly fades into the dark at dusk, you too can allow ease as you move through change. Today, spend some time considering areas of your life where you might be resisting change. Rather than fighting against the force of change, how can you allow the gift of surrender to make space for growth?

_____

_____

_____

_____

_____

_____

_____

_____

_____

_____

_____

_____

_____

_____

_____

_____

_____

_____

_____

_____

_____

_____

_____

_____

_____

_____

_____

_____

_____

_____

CHOOSE YOUR OWN PATH

A path is simply a clearing of space—a place where the footsteps of others have worn the ground down into a pattern that can be easily followed. Notice how each forked path offers its options equally. The path has no preference. It is up to you to choose which way you want to go, to decide which direction you will take. Today, know that just because a particular path has been worn down by many who have gone before you, that does not guarantee that it will lead you to your destination. Sometimes the first footsteps on the path to your goals will be your own. In the space provided, write about your path. Where have you been? Where are you going? Whom do you trust to come with you?

_____

_____

_____

_____

_____

_____

_____

_____

_____

CLEANSING RAIN

Find a place to sit quietly for a few minutes. Close your eyes, and imagine a rainstorm rolling in. Feel the experience of the storm surround you. Hear the loud claps of thunder. See the bright flashes of lightning. Listen for the pitter-patter of the raindrops on trees, the ground, and rocks. Imagine that this rain has come to cleanse you. Think of something that's causing you stress, and allow the raindrops to wash over you, taking your troubles along with them as they drip onto the ground. Use the space below to journal about what the rain washed away.

_____

_____

_____

_____

_____

_____

_____

_____

_____

_____

_____

NATURE'S SPECTRUM

Nature is full of examples of duality: Night and day. Birth and death. Hot and cold. Destruction and creation. Stillness and motion. But all of these realities exist on a continuum. Think about it—there are thousands of hues between bright light and total darkness, and millions of experiences between infancy and old age. It is within the polarities that we are able to observe the full spectrum of life's possibilities. Like nature, we as humans can be this, that, and everything in between. Today, find a quiet place to sit and consider something that appears black and white in your own life. Slowly envision the spectrum of thoughts, ideas, opinions, and realities that lie within this issue. In the stillness, imagine all the shades of truth that exist between these two seemingly opposite ideas. Journal about what comes up for you as you consider nature's spectrum.

_____

_____

_____

_____

_____

_____

_____

_____

_____

_____

_____

_____

_____

_____

_____

_____

_____

_____

CULTIVATING CALM

Sometimes life presents us with situations that challenge us and lead to difficult emotions. If we are not careful, those emotions can consume our hearts and govern our behavior. But just as nature eventually calms after a storm, we too have the ability to soothe ourselves following a challenging experience by using the power of our breath. Pause to imagine a situation that has been upsetting you. Think briefly about negative ideas, thoughts, and feelings associated with this situation. As you think of the situation, take a deep breath and hold it for a few seconds. Then, on your next exhale, release all you have been holding. Envision the negative feelings and emotions being expelled from your body on the waves of your breath. Allow yourself to experience the freedom of letting go, and remember that your breath is a tool you always have at your disposal. How did this exercise feel in your body? Your mind? What physical and mental sensations did you get while doing this?

_____

_____

_____

_____

_____

_____

LETTER FROM MY HIGH(EST) SELF

Physically changing our perspective by playing with elevation can help us see things in new ways.

ACTIVITY: Challenge yourself to complete a hike that includes gaining elevation. Choose a trail that will allow you to move from a lower point to a higher point. The elevation does not need to be dramatic, just a little higher than where you started. If your environment will not allow this, try sitting on top of a rock or stairs in an outdoor location. If you are unable to physically climb, consider taking an elevator to a higher point or driving to a lookout. The idea here is to notice the process of physically moving from a lower space to a higher space.

JOURNAL: From this place of perspective, consider what it might be like to be the highest version of yourself—the happiest, healthiest version of you. Spend some time really basking in that energy. Then, use this space to write a letter to yourself from the perspective of your highest self. What can your highest self offer you in this moment?

LETTER FROM MY HIGH(EST) SELF

WATERFALL OF WORTHINESS

Pride in ourselves and self-worth often go hand in hand. When we are feeling unworthy or need a confidence boost, accessing the memories of our greatest accomplishments can give us the courage and confidence we need. When our confidence is flowing like a waterfall, so is our faith in ourselves.

ACTIVITY: Visit a local waterfall. Observe the way the falling water cascades down into the pool or rapids below. Watch how the pressure of the water moves from crash to wave to ripple. If you can, dip your feet or hands into the water and imagine how far the drops you feel have traveled to meet you here. Then think of how many other people have been impacted by the beauty of this space. If you're unable to visit a waterfall, consider watching a video of a spectacular waterfall instead.

JOURNAL: From this place of appreciation, imagine yourself directly beneath a waterfall, the water rushing over you. Now imagine that the waterfall is spilling over with all your accomplishments and proudest moments. Bask in the feeling for as long as you'd like. Then use the space provided to make a list of all those moments and accomplishments. What flows from your waterfall of worthiness? How did it feel to feel those achievements wash over you?

_____

_____

_____

_____

_____

_____

_____

_____

_____

_____

_____

_____

_____

_____

_____

_____

WATERFALL OF WORTHINESS

LESSONS IN LEAVES

Even when you can't make it out into the natural world, you can still access its incredible power. This activity is something you can do almost anywhere—in bed, on a plane, or while you have your morning tea—and is a lovely way to ground yourself when you need a moment of calm.

ACTIVITY: Find a quiet, comfortable place to sit or lie and close your eyes. Take three deep cleansing breaths and relax your body. Begin to visualize a tree. A tree at the beginning of fall.

Picture the leaves on the tree, some of them green, others beginning to turn vibrant hues of orange and yellow and purple. Now focus on one leaf in particular. See every detail—the edges, curves, and stem.

Observe how this leaf blows as wind moves through the tree. Watch how it allows itself to be slowly rocked. Notice how it does not resist. The leaf knows no danger. No fear. Only blowing and flowing. From your position, imagine roots sprouting from your body and becoming connected to a strong foundation. Your limbs become like the leaves you envisioned. And each leaf represents an aspect of your life. Visualize the healthy green leaves as your hopes and dreams. They are strong and full of oxygen. Now imagine the orange, yellow, and purple ones. These leaves, while beautiful, are dying. They represent regret, hurts, and past pains. Feel the wind gently rustling these dying leaves.

Give thanks for the lessons that each of these leaves represents. Now, gratefully allow the lifeless ones to disconnect, drift, and fall away.

Continue to breathe here, and with each breath in, allow more oxygen to flow to the healthy lush leaves of your life. With each breath out, softly blow the leaves that no longer serve you off and away.

JOURNAL: What did you envision while doing this exercise? Which aspects of your life represented the green healthy leaves? Which aspects were represented by the orange, yellow, and purple leaves? Process your thoughts here.

walking thoughts

FINDING FOUNDATION

Earth is our home, providing us with everything we need to live and thrive. It is the foundation for everything we know—the food we eat, the people we love, the elements that nourish us. Take a short walk today, and as you move, feel the solid foundation of the earth beneath your feet and contemplate the other foundational elements of your life—the people, places, and experiences that ground you. When you return, use the space below to make a list of who and what makes you feel more grounded and supported. Next, make a list of who and what does not make you feel grounded or supported. Spend some time considering both lists, and then journal about what patterns, revelations, or emotions come up during your observations.

_____

_____

_____

_____

_____

_____

_____

_____

MINDFUL BEAUTY

Sometimes we walk on autopilot, arriving at our destination with-out much memory of the journey. When we stop paying attention to our surroundings, we miss moments of beauty and discovery. Today, take a short walk and challenge yourself to find beauty. It could be in the color of the sky, the patterns in the bark of a tree, or the sparkle in a rock. Even if you are looking at things you have seen before, make it a point to look closer, in an effort to observe something new. Use the space below to explore how you can apply this mindful attention to other parts of your life—especially parts of your life or self that may seem dull, ugly, or unworthy.

WALKING THOUGHTS

INVITE THE EVENING

Each evening, nature prepares for a night of rest. Flowers gently fold into themselves. Birdcalls begin to quiet. Living things settle into the peace of the night. Tonight, spend some time observing nature turning inward. Take a walk at dusk, or simply open a window to gaze at the sky. Then, from this place of quiet observation, contemplate what needs rest within you. How can you find inspiration in the slow evening rhythms of the natural world? What activities or rituals help you quiet your mind and body? Use the space below to journal about what makes you feel rested. How can you incorporate these things into a short wind-down routine each evening?

_____

_____

_____

_____

_____

_____

_____

_____

RETURN TO JOY

Nature is often the background for our most cherished memories—a game of hopscotch in the park with our friends, hide-and-go-seek in the woods, or maybe a camping trip with family. But as adults, we tend to see nature more as a vehicle for contemplation and personal transformation. It's important to remember, though, that it can also be a place for play, fun, and creativity. As you walk today, consider your earliest experiences with the outdoors and notice what comes up. Use the space below to record a favorite childhood experience in nature, then explore how you might tap into that same joyful energy as an adult.

_____

_____

_____

_____

_____

_____

_____

_____

FIND SWEET RELEASE

The natural world is constantly releasing pressure. When our oceans swell, waves lap onto our shores. When clouds get full, they release rain down onto the earth. When geysers overheat, they erupt with hot steam, radiating warmth. Today as you walk, see if you can find examples of nature releasing pressure, and spend some time contemplating pressure and release in your own life. Is there anything building up inside of you that is on the verge of exploding? How can you find moments of release? Use the space below to make a list of any conversations, activities, or decisions that will help you ease the pressure in your life. Then, pick one thing from your list to focus on this week.

_____

_____

_____

_____

_____

_____

_____

_____

PERSONAL PERSPECTIVE

Offering us perspective is one of nature's greatest gifts. Nature's splendor and enormity can help us bring our own small challenges and stressors into perspective. Today, spend some time walking outside and taking stock of your surroundings—whether it's the limitless sky, boundless rolling hills, enormous crashing waves, or a field of blooming flowers. How can nature's grandeur help you zoom out, away from the little things that bother you and toward something greater? Explore what comes up in the space below.

_____

_____

_____

_____

_____

_____

_____

_____

_____

_____

_____

_____

EMBRACING UNIQUENESS

Nature provides us with such marvelous examples of the beauty that comes from unique features: the awe-inspiring spiky rocks in Utah's Bryce Canyon National Park, the feathers of a peacock, and an entire crooked forest in Poland where trees grow at mind-bending angles. These occurrences remind us that our unique traits are often the things that make us beautiful, valuable, or appreciated. Today as you walk, examine how you may have judged yourself as imperfect, or different, and therefore flawed. Take stock of the toll that negative self-talk may have had on your self-image and self-esteem. Are there any ways in which you want to reframe your relationship with yourself? Journal about your thoughts.

_____

_____

_____

_____

_____

_____

_____

_____

_____

_____

_____

_____

_____

_____

_____

_____

_____

_____

_____

_____

TUNE IN TO INTUITION

If you've ever been lost in the outdoors, you know how frustrating it can be—it's disorienting, sometimes scary. But just as dolphins and whales can use echolocation and sonar to help them track their position, we can use intelligence and intuition to help us find our way. Today, as you walk, contemplate the areas of your life where you feel lost and may need to move in a new direction. Rather than continuing to wander aimlessly, consult your internal guidance system and see where your intuition directs you. Ask yourself what you need in order to get back on track. Journal about your answer below.

_____

_____

_____

_____

_____

_____

_____

_____

_____

_____

_____

WALKING THOUGHTS

UP FOR A CHALLENGE

Why do we challenge our bodies in nature? Some of us climb mountains in order to hear the sound of the earth beneath our feet and to savor the view when we reach the top. Others walk for the crispness of the fresh air that fills our lungs and for the heavy breaths that each step higher brings us. Some of us hike to feel our bodies grow stronger, celebrating the dull burn in our legs, backs, and feet as we move upward. And most of us do it to prove to ourselves that we can. When we challenge ourselves, we offer ourselves the chance to discover new parts of ourselves, expand our horizons, and experience the world beyond our comfort zones.

ACTIVITY: Plan a challenge hike or outdoor activity to push yourself a little. Make it a point to go farther or higher than you have before, or to do something new. That could mean going to a new place in the outdoors, picking a trail that is slightly more difficult than your previous hikes, or sleeping outside for the first time. Whatever you choose, make sure that it's safe and appropriate for your body and your level of experience. The goal here is not to do something enormously beyond your comfort level, but to gently challenge yourself and see what comes up when you do.

JOURNAL: Write about the experience below. What did you learn about yourself in the process? How might you apply that to other challenges in your life? How can you find pleasure and satisfaction in the journey?

HIKE TO HEAL

Hiking fosters unity with nature. As we move through the forest, traverse a trail, or summit a peak, our bodies become one with the earth beneath us. There are moments when our hearts beat in rhythm with the crunch of gravel underfoot as we feel both vulnerable and strong at the same time. Healing hikes can be a wonderful opportunity to tap into the powerfully restorative properties of the natural world.

ACTIVITY: Plan a healing hike: Plan a visit to a trail or outdoor space that you enjoy. As you walk, take deep breaths and bring your attention to the present moment, noticing your body, your breath, and the flora and fauna around you. As you move, imagine that you are connecting to the healing power of Mother Earth. With each step, envision yourself leaving behind whatever burdens you and picking up the tools that will strengthen and fortify you.

JOURNAL: Find a comfortable place to sit, somewhere along your walk (a grassy meadow, a park bench, a mountain summit, a bank of a river, a big rock, etc.). Once you are settled, reflect on what you have imagined and envisioned above, and allow your thoughts to flow onto the page. Once you've finished your journaling, close your eyes and thank yourself for showing up today—self-care is a practice.

QUALITY SHARE

There is something about spending time in the outdoors that allows for more thoughtful conversation and engagement. Sharing experiences in nature allows us to connect with friends and loved ones on a deeper level. One of the best ways to improve our relationship with anyone is to orient ourselves to the best parts of them.

ACTIVITY: Invite a friend, loved one, or coworker to join you in a hike, walk, or other outdoor activity. Instead of engaging in the usual conversation you might have with each other, be intentional about what you share with them. Use the following prompts as a conversation guide:

- Things I like most about you

- Things we share

- Things I would like to offer you

JOURNAL: When you've finished the conversation, spend some time unpacking what came up in the space provided. What surprised you? How did it feel to offer and receive praise? What will you take from the experience?

MAKE SPACE FOR PLAY

Play is proven to relieve stress, forge connections, and boost happiness. And playing in nature can take us back to a simpler and happier version of ourselves. Play is a beautiful way to connect with our inner child—the younger version of ourselves that we carry within us our entire lives, but often overlook.

ACTIVITY: Plan an outdoor play date for yourself and friends. Grab a Frisbee, jump rope, ball, or some chalk, and let your inner child shine. Go have fun for fun's sake only.

JOURNAL: Reflect on what it felt like to embrace and reconnect with your inner child through play. Then use the space provided to write a letter to your younger self. What messages do you want them to hear? What lessons do you want to share? What do you hope for for them?

messages from the earth

HONOR YOUR ECOSYSTEM

A healthy ecosystem is a network of interconnected beings working together. Within an ecosystem, every living thing—big or small—plays an important role in maintaining the balance of the environment. Similarly, in our personal lives, we all have things that contribute to a healthy, balanced state of mind. Today, spend some time meditating on an ecosystem in the natural world, and imagine it in as much detail as possible—the plants, bodies of water, animals, insects, and more that work together. Now consider your own spiritual ecosystem with the same level of care and attention. Below, make a list of at least ten practices, rituals, or relationships that support your personal growth and help you to cultivate a happy, healthy mind. Return to this list whenever your personal ecosystem is out of alignment, and reconnect with the items on the list to help you restore a healthy balance.

_____

_____

_____

_____

_____

_____

_____

_____

_____

_____

_____

_____

_____

_____

_____

_____

_____

_____

_____

_____

_____

_____

_____

_____

_____

HONOR YOUR ECOSYSTEM

THRIVING NOT SURVIVING

A cactus can thrive in the desert. The hot, dry climate is exactly what it needs to grow and flourish. A redwood tree, however, would perish in that environment. Like plants, individuals need specific things to make them comfortable and happy. Today, identify three to five things that you need in order to prosper in your environment. What are those things? Why are they so important to you?

_____

_____

_____

_____

_____

_____

_____

_____

_____

_____

_____

HEED THE ALARM

In the natural world, there are almost always warning signs that forecast extreme conditions. Thunder alerts us to rain, high winds signal hurricanes, and tremors beneath our feet forecast quakes in the earth. And while humans may not see literal lightning flashes before something bad happens, we do have internal alarms. We get gut feelings or bad vibes, and we sense strange energy when something is "off" about a situation or person. Spend some time thinking about the spaces and people that you interact with on a regular basis in your daily life. Notice what sorts of signals your body gives you when you interact with different people or spaces. What is your internal barometer trying to tell you? Are there any signs you have been ignoring? Reflect below.

_____

_____

_____

_____

_____

_____

_____

_____

_____

THE LITTLE VICTORIES

Spending time in the natural world is full of little victories—the satisfaction of pushing our bodies, demonstrating leadership, summiting new peaks. Each and every day holds the possibility of a small personal victory—a moment of triumph that can help us build confidence. If you're not paying attention, however, you may miss them. Today as you walk, identify a personal victory you had recently. It could be something you learned, something new you tried, or something difficult you overcame. What little victory can you celebrate today? Use the space below to reflect on the experience and explore what you can carry with you from that small win.

_____

_____

_____

_____

_____

_____

_____

_____

_____

_____

_____

CELEBRATE COOPERATIVE PURPOSE

Everything in nature has a purpose. Bees pollinate our plants. Ants aerate our soil. Trees release oxygen. Each organism works independently for the good of the collective. As a part of our whole, you too have a unique and special contribution to make to our planet. Today, consider what your role is in your own ecosystem— be it home life, school, or work—and how your purpose benefits the collective. Celebrate all the ways in which you add value to the spaces you occupy. What comes up for you when you think about your purpose?

_____

_____

_____

_____

_____

_____

_____

_____

_____

_____

PRESSURE AND PREPARATION

It can take more than a billion years for a diamond to form. Made from carbon deposits found deep within the earth, diamonds only materialize after millions of years of intense pressure. The process is long, but the result is precious. Today, know that in life each of us will have moments of pressure and preparation. Understand that sometimes those moments are necessary in order to give birth to something greater. Then contemplate a past or present experience in which an unpleasant situation transformed you over time. What did this experience teach you?

_____

_____

_____

_____

_____

_____

_____

_____

_____

_____

_____

_____

_____

_____

EMBRACE ABUNDANCE

We live in a universe of abundance, yet many of us operate from a scarcity mindset. We worry that we won't have "enough" and feel jealous of what other people seem to have. But the most valuable things on Earth—the air that we breathe, the forests that clean our atmosphere, the oceans that sustain our planet—are free. Today, spend some time outside and take note of the abundance around you. Whether you're at the beach, walking through the woods, or sitting in a local park, celebrate nature's abundance and know that there is more than enough for you here on Earth. In the space provided, journal about times when you've approached things from a scarcity mindset. How might your perspective or decisions change if you took another look at the situation or experience from a mindset of abundance?

_____

_____

_____

_____

_____

_____

_____

_____

_____

_____

_____

_____

_____

_____

_____

_____

_____

_____

_____

_____

_____

_____

_____

_____

_____

TAKE FLIGHT

It is not uncommon to see baby birds attempting flight after only days of life. Even though their legs are wobbly and their wings are very freshly formed, they leap, jump, and dive. All in an attempt to do what comes naturally to them. For them, flying is an instinct, even before it is a skill. Today, know that where baby birds have instincts, you have intuition. It is the quiet voice that whispers to you, "You are ready"—even amid your physical or emotional insecurity. Think of a situation in your life where you feel "led" but "lacking" in some way. How can you tap into the inner wisdom of your intuition to take the leap that is needed? What would need to be in place for you to feel more confident?

_____

_____

_____

_____

_____

_____

_____

_____

EMBRACE THE ELEMENTS

Earth, air, wind, and fire are the building blocks of our world. They create the framework for our sensory experiences and the platform for our physical reality. In this activity, you will spend time considering these four elements and how they relate to your emotional and mental state.

ACTIVITY: Plan to visit a space where you can experience each element—a local park, a nearby beach, a hike that follows a creek. Bring a stick of incense or a candle to light during your visit or, if you're feeling more ambitious, you could even build a small campfire (make sure to follow local regulations). Spend some time bringing your senses to each element. Take note of the sensory experience and of any emotions that come up while your attention is focused on the elements.

JOURNAL: Make a list of the elements and write about what imagery, emotions, thoughts, or sensations arise in connection with earth, air, wind, and fire.

MESSAGES FROM THE EARTH

MEET THE MORNING

The natural world greets each new morning with renewed energy—flowers bloom open, roosters crow, lizards crawl out into the warm sunlight. Indeed, everything has a special and unique way of waking up to the world. Observing nature welcoming a new day can set a beautiful tone for our own daily routine.

ACTIVITY: Plan a sunrise hike. Figure out what time the sun will rise and plan a hike or nature walk that corresponds with it. As you observe the world transition from darkness to dawn, think of the possibility that is present in each new day.

JOURNAL: How can you organize your mornings so that you greet the day with energy and positivity? Consider what rituals or routines you can establish to make your mornings more peaceful and purposeful. Do you want to watch the sun rise? Meditate and listen to the birds chirping? Take an early morning walk? Record your new or current morning routine in the space provided. If you don't have a routine, use this space to create one. How do you want to meet your mornings?

strengthening affirmations

CREATE YOUR OWN CONDITIONS

Plants and animals don't wait for the perfect conditions to come to them. Salmon put a lot of effort into swimming upstream to spawn. A sapling will bend and contort itself to find its way toward sunlight. Gray whales swim from the oceans of the Arctic to Central America each year to find food. Consider the parts of your life in which you're waiting for opportunity to fall into your lap, and spend some time meditating on the phrase "I can create my own conditions." When you're finished, make a list of the things that need to be in place for you to feel comfortable pursuing this goal. Read through the list and then pick three things that you can commit to working on immediately.

_____

_____

_____

_____

_____

_____

_____

_____

_____

_____

_____

_____

_____

_____

_____

_____

_____

_____

_____

_____

_____

_____

_____

_____

STRENGTHENING AFFIRMATIONS

_____

_____

_____

_____

_____

_____

_____

_____

_____

_____

_____

_____

_____

_____

_____

_____

_____

_____

_____

CREATE YOUR OWN CONDITIONS

STRENGTHENING AFFIRMATIONS

SURVEY YOUR SHADOW

Close your eyes and imagine standing with the sun at your back, your shadow cast in front of you on the ground. This shadow represents the parts of yourself that you avoid—the challenging emotions, the difficult memories. Our shadows are a part of us, traveling with us and mirroring our every move, reminding us that there's no separation between our darkness and our light. Your shadow is evidence of your solidity, your presence in our universe. It proves that you are whole. Spend some time sitting with the phrase "I accept my shadow." Then, in the space below, journal about what comes up for you. What parts of yourself are you hiding from the world? What lessons can your shadow teach you? What does it feel like to acknowledge your shadow?

_____

_____

_____

_____

_____

_____

_____

_____

STRENGTHENING AFFIRMATIONS

PERSONAL BEAUTY

For some of us, the word *beauty* elicits feelings of comparison, inadequacy, and insecurity. It's easy to focus on our flaws as we measure ourselves against other people. But nature teaches us that there is more than one way to be beautiful, and that the presence of beauty in another does not detract from our own. From blooming flowers to vivid sunsets to spectacular waterfalls, there are countless ways to be beautiful. Today, pick one thing that you find beautiful in nature—a tree, an animal, a flower, a vista—and take note of all the details that make it beautiful. What would it feel like to bring that same level of care and attention to the attributes that make you uniquely beautiful? In your head or out loud, say the phrase "I am beautiful in my own way." Then use the space below to journal about what this brings up for you. What makes you beautiful in your own unique way? How does it feel to turn your attention to the beautiful parts of your mind, body, and spirit?

_____

_____

_____

_____

_____

_____

_____

_____

_____

_____

_____

_____

_____

_____

_____

_____

_____

_____

_____

_____

_____

_____

_____

_____

STRENGTHENING AFFIRMATIONS

STRENGTHENING AFFIRMATIONS

TAKE THE SPACE YOU NEED

Trees are only as strong and healthy as their root system. Roots provide stability and deliver the nourishment and water essential to the tree's survival. A tree's roots can extend hundreds of feet out into the surrounding soil, carving pathways through sidewalks, curbs, and over other trees, and taking up whatever space they need to support themselves. Today, imagine yourself as a tree putting down roots and quietly speak the phrase "I will take the space that I need." From this place of confidence, journal about a place in your life where you have been playing small and need to take up more space. How can you show up differently?

_____

_____

_____

_____

_____

_____

_____

_____

_____

_____

STRENGTHENING AFFIRMATIONS

NOURISH THE SEEDS

Seeds hold potential for new life within their small structures. But without the proper nourishment—the right amount of light, water, and nutrients—a seed will not yield life. Today, focus on something you want to accomplish—a creative idea, a personal project, a long-term goal—and consider what kind of resources and support it needs to succeed. Then close your eyes and commit to seeking those things as you repeat the phrase, "I will nourish what I want to see grow." Journal about the things that you want to see grow in your life, and how will you nourish them, in the space provided.

_____

_____

_____

_____

_____

_____

_____

_____

STRENGTHENING AFFIRMATIONS

CHANGE IS OPPORTUNITY

Change can cause suffering. We suffer when our plans don't come together as we expected, when a relationship ends, or when we have to uproot our lives for one reason or another. But in the midst of the pain, there is also so much potential for joy and opportunity. When you feel your heart resisting inevitable change, visualize a tree moving through the seasons—turning red and gold in autumn, shedding its leaves in winter, growing new buds in spring, and showing its glorious greenery in summer. Consider how you can move through the ebbs and flows of the seasons in your own life with the grace of a tree and repeat this affirmation: "Change is full of opportunity." Explore the idea of change as opportunity in the space below. How are you changing? What stage of evolution are you in?

_____

_____

_____

_____

_____

_____

_____

_____

STRENGTHENING AFFIRMATIONS

CHANGE IS OPPORTUNITY

_____

_____

_____

_____

_____

_____

_____

_____

_____

_____

_____

_____

_____

_____

_____

_____

_____

STRENGTHENING AFFIRMATIONS

FLOAT AND FLOW

There is a difference between surrendering and giving up. Surrender means choosing to release something and entering a state of flow. Have you ever watched leaves being blown around by the breeze? They surrender to the wind and simply float along on the air's current, moving in whatever direction the wind carries them. When we choose to "go with the flow," we give up the pain that comes from resisting the winds of change and embrace the natural trajectory of our journey. Today, consider an area of resistance in your own life. Close your eyes and repeat, "I will float and flow." Use the space below to consider places in your life where you might surrender to the flow. Imagine what it would feel like to stop fighting and instead choose to float like a leaf on the wind.

_____

_____

_____

_____

_____

_____

_____

_____

STRENGTHENING AFFIRMATIONS

HONOR THE CYCLE OF LIFE

Death is an inevitable part of the cycle of life, a natural shift from one state of being to another. It's a process that every living being must go through. But death does not mean the absolute end of something. As living beings, we all carry on in different ways, even when we're no longer alive. Our ideas, our love, our shared memories, and our work here on Earth live on through future generations. As we grieve, we also remember. The following activities are designed to help you celebrate those no longer with us, turning your memories of them into inspiration while also basking in the healing properties of the natural world.

ACTIVITY: A mile for _____ (insert the name of a lost loved one). Plan a one-mile walk, bike ride, or hike in memory of someone who has passed on. As you move, dedicate your steps or pedaling to your loved one. Hold them in your thoughts. Call to mind happy memories. Move with love and intention.

JOURNAL: Grief journaling can be a beautiful way to remember those who have passed on and a powerful way to process emotions. Today, find a place to sit outside or with a view of the outdoors, and pause to think of your favorite memories of this person. What did you love to do with them? What reminds you of them? What music comes to mind when you think of them? What is one thing they taught you? If it feels right, consider ending your entry by completing the sentence "I will honor you by . . ." And commit to at least one way of celebrating your loved one.

STRENGTHENING AFFIRMATIONS

_____

_____

_____

_____

_____

_____

_____

_____

_____

_____

_____

_____

_____

_____

_____

_____

_____

STRENGTHENING AFFIRMATIONS

WRITE YOUR OWN NATURE AFFIRMATION

Affirmations are positive phrases that help you reprogram your mind. They can be a single word, a short statement, or something longer. Affirmations are spoken, and often repeated, in order to aid in meditation and mindfulness activities, serving as a reminder of what we want to focus on and/or manifest in our lives. Affirmations can be inspired by anything: experiences we want to have, ways we want to feel, resources we want to attract, or qualities we want to emulate.

ACTIVITY: For this activity you are asked to consider an aspect of nature that you are grateful for and use it to inspire an affirmation. Pick something in your local natural environment that brings you joy, peace, or calm—maybe it's the ocean, or the tall trees in your neighborhood park, or the sunset. Make it a point to spend time contemplating this natural feature or phenomena and consider how it enriches your life. What emotions does it bring up? Spend some moments observing it in as much detail as possible. Let everything else go.

JOURNAL: From this place of contemplation and admiration, reflect on your gratitude and write an affirmation inspired by this natural feature. What are its positive qualities that you want to embody, and how does it enrich your life? For example, this might look like:

I AM GRATEFUL FOR: The beauty of the sunrise. This enriches my life because it reminds me that every day starts off with beauty and possibility.

STRENGTHENING AFFIRMATION: I am radiant and beautiful like the rising sun.

Return to your nature affirmation whenever you are in need of confidence or inspiration.

WRITE YOUR OWN NATURE AFFIRMATION

_____

_____

_____

_____

_____

_____

_____

_____

_____

_____

_____

_____

_____

_____

_____

_____

_____

_____

STRENGTHENING AFFIRMATIONS

WRITE YOUR OWN NATURE AFFIRMATION